1997

BUSINESS
ITALY

D1571391

BUSINESS ITALY

A Practical Guide to Understanding Italian Business Culture

Peggy Kenna   **Sondra Lacy**

PASSPORT BOOKS
a division of *NTC Publishing Group*
Lincolnwood, Illinois USA

Library of Congress Cataloging-in-Publication Data

Kenna, Peggy.
    Business Italy: a practical guide to understanding Italian
business culture / Peggy Kenna, Sondra Lacy.
        p. cm.
    ISBN 0-8442-3557-1
    1. Business etiquette—Italy. 2. Corporate culture—Italy. 3.
    Business communication—Italy. 4. Negotiation in business—Italy.
    I. Lacy, Sondra. II. Title.
HF5389.K4545 1995
395'.52'0945--dc20   94-16181
                          CIP

Published by Passport Books, a division of NTC Publishing Group.
4255 West Touhy Avenue, Lincolnwood, (Chicago), Illinois 60646-1975 U.S.A.
© 1995 by NTC Publishing Group All rights reserved.
No part of this book may be reproduced, stored in a retrieval system,
or transmitted in any form or by any means,
electronic, mechanical, photocopying, recording or otherwise,
without the prior permission of NTC Publishing Group.
Manufactured in the United States of America.

4 5 6 7 8 9 0 VP 9 8 7 6 5 4 3 2 1

Contents

Peggy Kenna is a communication specialist working with foreign-born professionals in the American workplace. She provides cross-cultural training and consultation services to companies who are conducting business internationally. She is also a certified speech and language pathologist who specializes in accent modification. Peggy lives in Tempe, Arizona.

Sondra Lacy is a certified communications specialist and teaches American communication skills to foreign-born professionals in the American workplace. She also provides cross-cultural training and consultation services to companies conducting business internationally. Sondra lives in Scottsdale, Arizona.

Business Italy is an invaluable tool for thousands of entrepreneurs, businesspeople, corporate executives, technicians, and salespeople seeking to develop lasting business relationships in italy.

The book provides a fast, easy way for you to become acquainted with business practices and protocol so you can increase your chances for success in Italy. You will discover the secrets of doing business internationally while improving your interpersonal communication skills.

Let this book work for you.

> Pam Del Duca
> President/CEO
> The DELSTAR Group
> Scottsdale, Arizona

Business Italy offers a smooth and problem-free transition between the American and Italian business cultures.

This pocket-size book contains information you need when traveling in Italy or doing business with Italian colleagues. It explains the differences in business culture you will encounter in such areas as:

- Business etiquette

- Communication style

- Problem solving and decision making

- Meetings and presentation style

Business Italy gets you started on the right track and challenges you to seek ways to improve your success in the global marketplace by understanding cultural differences in the ways people communicate and do business with each other.

Successful international companies are able to adapt to the business styles acceptable in other countries and by other nationalities, based on their knowledge and awareness of key cultural differences. These differences, if not acknowledged and addressed, can interfere in successful communication and can adversely affect the success of any business attempting to expand internationally.

Business Italy is designed to overcome such difficulties by comparing the American culture with the culture of Italy. Identifying appropriate behavior in one's own culture can make it easier to adapt to that of the country with which you are doing business. With this in mind, the book's unique parallel layout allows an at-a-glance comparison of Italian business practices with those of the United States.

Practical and easy to use, *Business Italy* will help you win the confidence of Italian associates and achieve common business goals.

The Global Marketplace

The global business environment today is a multi-cultural one. While general business considerations are essentially the same the world over, business styles differ greatly from country to country.

What is customary and appropriate in one country may be considered unusual or even offensive in another. The increasingly competitive environment calls for an individual approach to each national market. The success of your venture outside your home market depends largely upon preparation. The American style of business is not universally accepted. Yet we send our employees, executives, salespeople, technicians to negotiate or carry out contracts with little or no understanding of the cultural differences in the ways people communicate and do business with each other. How many business deals have been lost because of this cultural myopia?

Globalization is a process which is drawing people together from all nations of the world into a single community linked by the vast network of communication technologies. Technological breakthroughs in the past two decades have made instant communication between individuals around the world an affordable reality.

As these technological advances continue to open up and expand the dialogue among members of the world community, the need for effective communication between nations and peoples has accelerated.

When change occurs as dramatically and rapidly as we have witnessed in the past decade, many people throughout the world are being forced to quickly learn and adapt to unfamiliar ways of doing things. Some actually welcome change and the opportunities it presents, while others are reluctant to give up familiar ways of doing things. History proves that cultures are slow to change. But, individuals who are mentally prepared to accept change and deal with differences can successfully adapt to cultures very different from their own.

A culture develops when individuals have common experiences and share their reactions to these experiences by communicating with other members of their society.

Over time, communication becomes the vehicle by which cultural beliefs and values are developed, shared and transmitted from one generation to the next. Communication and culture are mutually dependent.

Effective communication between governments or international businesses requires more than being able to speak the language fluently or relying on expert interpreters. Understanding the language is only the first step. Understanding and accepting the behaviors, customs and attitudes of other cultures is also required to bring harmony and success in the worldwide business and political arena.

The importance of the influence of one's native culture on the way one approaches life cannot be overstated. Each country's cultural beliefs and values are reflected in its people's idea of the "right" way to live and behave.

In general, businesspeople who practice low-key, non-adversarial, win/win techniques in doing business abroad tend to be most successful. Knowing what your company wants to achieve, its bottom line, and also understanding the objectives of the other party and helping to accommodate them in the business transaction is necessary for developing long-term, international business relationships.

Often, representatives from American companies, for example, have difficulty doing business with *each other*, even when they speak the same language and share a common culture. Consider how much more difficult it is to do business with people from different cultures who speak different languages.

Success in the international business arena will not be easy for those who do not take steps to gain the skills necessary to be a global player. The language barrier is an obvious problem.

Equally important will be negotiation skills, as well as an understanding of and adaptation to the social and business etiquette of the foreign country. Americans have a reputation for failing to appreciate this. In other words, businesspeople doing business abroad will get off to a good start if they remember to do the following:

- Listen closely; understand the verbal and non-verbal communications.
- Focus on mutual interests, not differences.
- Nurture long-term relationships
- Emphasize quality. Be prepared to defend the quality of your products and services, and the quality of your business relationship.

ISO 9000 is fast becoming a universal passport for doing business in Europe. ISO stands for International Organization for Standardization.

This is a new set of concise standards covering documented quality control systems for product development, design, production, management and inspection.

The European Economic Community (EEC) has adopted ISO certification and more than 20,000 European companies are complying. Increasing numbers of European companies are refusing to do business with foreign suppliers who don't meet ISO standards. Product areas under the most pressure to comply include automotive, aerospace, electronics, testing and measuring instruments, and products where reliability and safety can become an issue. Companies with Total Quality Management (TQM) in place find it easier to pass ISO 9000 audits.

Successful American companies will need to adapt to these rules and standards set by Europe in order to do business there.

Total Quality Management is becoming an integral part of successful companies in the United States.

TQM is an organized, company-wide effort to eliminate waste in every aspect of business and to produce the highest quality product possible. TQM is a philosophy that focuses on the customer, manages by facts, empowers people and improves processes.

Implementation of TQM is a real challenge and requires a company commitment to invest the time and finances necessary to reshape the entire organization. How is this accomplished? Through a team approach which values customer and employee opinions and in which everyone is committed to identify waste and its root cause and correct it in a timely manner. An effective tool for accomplishing this is through brainstorming efforts that allow everyone to participate. The successful TQM company is customer driven and uses leadership, information and analysis, strategic quality planning, human resource utilization and quality assurance of products and services to reach goals.

Total Quality Management is a survival tool for American businesses in a global market.

Cultural achievement is the main source of Italian pride. They are very proud of their culture and heritage and most are knowledgeable about European history, culture and languages. They value creativity and like new ideas and new ways of doing things.

Italian people have a reputation for valuing the arts, culture and an easygoing lifestyle. Italians are also very conscious and proud of their past. Visible reminders are everywhere for them. Italy has found it a long and difficult experience to turn itself into a moderately modern country.

Italy has 57 million people and one of the larger economies in Europe. It is one of the original six countries in the European Economic Union.

Italy is roughly divided into the industrialized north and the underdeveloped south. The two regions have very different attitudes towards work. Italian history over the past 3,000 years has included many races and cultures that crossed over the borders of what is now France, Switzerland, Austria and Yugoslavia. The main immigration came from the seas that surround Italy. Northern Italians will be more like Northern Europeans whereas Southern Italians will be more like Greek or Arabian people.

Italy is a matrix of interests and loyalties. All aspects of Italian life are dominated by rival interest groups. Affiliation with a group is essential for many Italians. The most important affiliation is the family. The family is the core of everything. Italians believe that trust, loyalty and personal relationships are very important and won't do business until they are certain of the quality of the people they working with.

The exercise of power is very obscure. The Italians love pomp and ceremony but this gives no indication as to who really has power. Very little is done "by the book"; rules are often evaded.

Status depends on birth and class, not wealth. It is almost impossible to change one's status.

Italy has a very active underground economy. There are a large number of small family-owned businesses. These businesses usually like long-term planning and it is not uncommon to find that they have business plans that cover up to fifty years. They are farsighted and run their businesses through tough family control. Regulation of business is minimal. There are also a number of very large companies.

Italy is very dependent on foreign trade and thus has very liberal investment policies. The government has encouraged foreign investment as the avenue to economic growth, greater employment and technological advancement.

The Catholic Church is also a very visible and active part of the Italian political scene. The power of the Church is less in sophisticated urban areas than in the more rural areas. The Church has little influence on ethics and morals in business.

Italy has the 12th largest economy in Europe but only 36% of its workforce are female (in the United States it is over 50%). As in many countries, few women are in decision-making positions. There are a few companies, however, which are run by women whose families own the company. These women are sophisticated, well-to-do, polished in their social and professional skills, and very powerful.

Italians are not as apt to speak English as are Northern Europeans, so it is advisable to provide yourself with a translator.

Italy's conservative Christian Democratic party has ruled for the past 50 years and made Italy one of the most stable democratic countries in Europe. However, recently massive corruption scandals have produced enormous changes in Italian politics.

The uncertainty of the political situation has threatened the stability of the financial markets in Italy. So anyone planning to do business there should do some research ahead of time.

Remember that within every culture there are still individual differences among people and organizations. Be prepared to find specific exceptions to the general trends within a culture.

United States

■ *Straightforward*

Americans value being candid, direct, forthright and open. They distrust ambiguousness and feel it is an attempt to hide something. American managers tend to share information much more freely and have a less autocratic style.

■ *More reserved*

Americans tend to be assertive and like to bargain hard but they believe that emotions should be kept out of the process.

■ *Be clear, logical and firm*

Americans like people to present their ideas clearly, logically, concisely and to defend their position firmly.

■ *Indirect and complicated*

Facts are secretly guarded and traded on a transactional basis. Many Italians believe there are powerful personalities or organizations dominating everything.

■ *Demonstrative and emotional*

Italians can become very loud and emotional during stressful negotiations. They may display great disappointment when desired concessions are not made.

Italians tend to be very volatile and when conversing, gesticulate wildly. To others, they may look like they are ready to come to blows, but in reality they may be only having a stimulating conversation.

■ *Be clear and rational*

Italians like people who present their ideas clearly and rationally and show a great deal of confidence. Italians also love to argue and can easily get a speaker off the track or let a meeting get too emotional.

Communication Style

United States

■ *Joking is common*

Americans feel joking relieves stress and keeps relations informal and friendly; therefore they often use jokes during informal business meetings.

Americans rarely use jokes during a formal presentation and rarely socialize after business has been conducted.

■ *Direct and to the point*

Americans prefer people to say what they mean; they tend to sometimes miss nonverbal cues. Americans also tend to be uncomfortable with ambiguousness; they don't like to have to "fill in the blanks." American also expect people to perform as they say they will and non-performance will bring a negative reaction.

■ *Style is important*

Italians value wit, humor and good spirits. This is particularly important when socializing after business. It is not as evident during business meetings. However, socializing after business has been conducted is vital to future success.

Italians can be very charming, even when telling you no. They like to make entrances and exits with a flourish, eat and drink well and talk about their families with pride.

■ *Ambiguous*

Italian words seldom mean exactly what they seem to mean. The listener must "read between the lines." It is vital when doing business with Italians to ensure your Italian counterpart understands any agreement the same way you do and also understands the consequences of non-performance.

United States

■ *Decision makers at all levels*

One person is usually given power to make the final decision and bear all responsibility. Major decisions tend to go from the top down. Decision makers can be found at all levels, however, depending on the importance of the decision. Lower level managers often get a chance to provide input; Americans believe that those closest to a problem should have input in determining the solution.

■ *Procedures oriented*

Americans like direct specific work orders. Each person has a well-defined function in a company. They are uneasy with ambiguity and hidden hierarchies. They like to have outlined exactly what is to be done. A person's credibility at work is determined by their technical competence and their ability to play by the rules of the company's game plan.

■ *Decision maker hard to find*

Decision making is usually concentrated with one executive or, at most, a few. Management is a top-down process.

The conventional hierarchy is found only at the lower levels in a large company. At the upper levels of management, alliances are built on personal relationships. Finding a decision maker can be difficult — he or she may not even be a part of the organizational structure. Many times the decision maker is remote and yet must approve any final agreement.

■ *Flexibility valued*

Italian managers value pragmatism and improvisation. They have a strong tendency to ignore procedures and place their trust in specific individuals to get things done. This can make them seem volatile at times.

The amount of confidence and trust Italians give depends on the respect they have for that person.

United States

■ *Leaders set overall direction*

While decisions can be made at all levels, the major direction of a company is determined at the top.

Implementation is delegated downward. Written policies and procedures are common. Feedback on implementation of policies and procedures is essential for efficient operations.

■ *Majority rules*

Americans expect everyone to express their opinions openly. A complete consensus is not required; dissenters will give way to the majority.

■ *Leader controls and implements*

Good leaders are seen as a parent figure. Their responsibility is implementation and control, not decision making or planning. Written policies and procedures are rare. Leadership is by example. Executives tend to be autocratic and this includes their dealings with outsiders.

There is often little delegation of authority by management and communication in the larger companies can often leave something to be desired. There is not much feedback between superiors and subordinates, even at management level.

■ *Consensus necessary*

Italians don't readily take instructions. It is important to first build consensus and obtain their commitment to your ideas. Positions are often hotly contested before this consensus is achieved. Persuasion, persistence and follow-up is essential. It is vital all parties to an agreement understand the agreement and commit themselves to implementing it.

Sometimes, executives in smaller and mid-sized companies will make subjective decisions based on their impressions rather than on gathering facts or building consensus among their managers.

United States

■ *Legal agreements*

Americans like to spell out all contingencies. And the contract is expected to be followed completely. Any changes must be agreed to by all parties.

■ *Trust more readily*

Business relationships are not seen as being personal. Americans tend to trust other people until they find themselves proved wrong.

Once trust is broken, credibility is difficult to restore.

■ *Legal agreements*

Italians like to reach a balance of power between parties. Achieving a win-win situation is important. They also tend to obey only the laws they personally find just and useful. They are very selective in how they interpret a contract and which parts they believe are important and will make a strong effort to follow.

■ *Trust must be earned*

Italians believe that trust is very important and is something that can be built only over time. Primarily trust goes to the family.

Gaining their trust is essential to doing business with them; this is absolutely critical to successfully doing business in Italy. Gaining this trust means building a personal relationship and this takes time. Italians like to do business with people they know well.

United States

■ *Planning*

Americans are both strategic and tactical planners. Contracts are written, detailed and not flexible; they must be renegotiated to be changed. Planning tends to be short term.

■ *Believe in preparation*

Americans spend time and effort planning concepts and establishing procedures to carry out the plan. Success or failure is dependent on the agreed to plan.

■ *Pragmatic*

Americans value people who are both resourceful and practical. They go with what will work. They value businesslike and effective solutions to problems.

■ *Forecasting and planning*

Italians rarely have a written strategic plan. They tend to thrive on ambiguity and risk. They like to identify and exploit a niche without waiting or doing an in-depth analysis.

Impromptu management decisions are often made without much advance preparation or research.

■ *Improvisation valued*

Italians value vitality and creativity. They therefore give themselves much freedom to depart from the agreed-upon plan. They tend to see rules in business as guidelines only.

Italian organizations tend to like protocol and status. They are also very sensitive to perceived insults.

■ *Inventive and imaginative*

Italians are always looking for new ways of doing things, for ways to evade the existing rules. This can make them appear to be very disorganized at times. They tend to be very creative and flamboyant in their approach to problem solving.

Organizational Structure

United States

■ *Relationships short term*

To Americans, business relationships are not personal. They tend to trust the other party until they have been proved wrong. Americans also tend to have little problem meeting strangers but usually do not develop long-term social and personal relationships with people they do business with.

■ *Power*

Power is not always determined by title or education; it can be determined by personality, money and political savvy. There is personal power as well as position power. People with charisma are the ones with personal power while position power is determined by the hierarchy. When both position power and personal power are combined, that person is usually a very powerful leadership figure.

■ *Build relationships*

A contractual relationship is not enough. Italians want a relationship based on honor in which everyone visibly profits. They will then give their total cooperation and commitment. If a business partner does not establish this type of relationship, Italians can be highly competitive and argumentative. Informal associations and alliances are the real basis of the organization.

■ *Power*

Italians do not see power as something equally shared among peers. They have class distinctions based on titles. Power is based on things like family background and hierarchy is very important.

Punctuality

United States

■ *Punctuality important*

Americans are very schedule oriented. They believe in accomplishing a job with a minimum expenditure of time. Efficiency is important. Meetings are expected to start on time and end on time. Americans do not like to waste time.

■ *Time is fluid*

Deliberate lateness is considered rude; however, Italians see time as fairly fluid. They have a very relaxed attitude about time. It is impolite to arrive late but even more impolite to break off a previous meeting because it is running over. Adhering to a schedule is rare. They feel things can usually wait until later.

It is advisable to make appointments well in advance.

United States

■ *Communication tool*

Some meetings are brainstorming sessions; some are to disseminate information; some are to discuss, defend and decide.

Americans like fixed agendas and schedules. They want to get down to business immediately since time is so important. A meeting may be adjourned before all business is completed but they always leave with some kind of action plan.

Meetings can become very heated with confrontations and disagreements to be resolved.

Although business meetings always include cordial greetings, little time is spent socializing.

■ *Unstructured and informal*

The purpose of meetings is to evaluate the mood of others, sense supporters and "test the water," to pool information or talk about problems. Impromptu side meetings are not uncommon.

An agenda is difficult to impose. Italians have a tendency to analyze extensively. Many see meetings as a stage for exhibiting their eloquence, performance, status and to see how far they can influence the final decision. Results may be less tangible than in American meetings. Participants mostly want to get a general idea of where things are going.

The weight given to an idea may be determined by the importance and influence of the person proposing the idea. The hierarchy may be more important than the idea.

Important decisions are not usually made during meetings. Any decisions agreed to in meetings may not be implemented "to the letter" since participants may have felt coerced to agree. Italians' contributions tend to be innovative, complex, creative and stimulating — and not always relevant.

Preliminary social talk is less important in Northern Italy than in the South.

United States

■ *Presentations*

Americans tend to have a projecting style of presentation. They will often combine informative and persuasive styles as an efficient method of presentation. They attempt to persuade the audience to make a decision or take an action at the same time as they provide information. They consider this an effective and efficient use of time. Americans also believe in the "hard sell" and "quick close" approach to selling. They expect the audience to ask questions at the end of a formal presentation and to test the presenter's knowledge. Presenters expect to defend their opinions.

■ *Presentations*

Formal presentations are not common in Italian companies.

Italians like presentations to be factual, detailed, logical, orderly, concise and to include charts and graphs whenever possible. Presentations should also include relevance to local applications.

They like people who use a calm approach and a soft sell. They also like presenters who project an air of confidence in themselves and in their product.

Style is very important to Italians. A polished and elegant presentation is very appreciated. It is best for Americans to watch their use of gestures when giving a presentation since gestures can mean very different things in different countries.

Italians are also used to interrupting frequently. Emotional outbursts are accepted as common-place business tactics to Italians. This can some-times sound autocratic and manipulative to for-eigners. Italians have few formal rules of debate so meetings can sometimes seem like a free-for-all.

United States

■ *Direct and open*

Americans tend to be very open and direct in their communication. They like to deal with differences directly and tend to "lay their cards on the table" in order to resolve issues.

■ *Task oriented*

Americans are highly task oriented. They are good at taking responsibility and getting things done. They are more interested in the technical aspects of negotiation than in building relationships. Americans like to get down to business right away and do not worry about establishing a relationship. Money is often an end in itself.

Americans have typically negotiated from a win/lose standpoint. They feel someone wins and someone loses.

■ *Contracts*

Americans are legalistic and like detailed contracts with all contingencies spelled out. These contracts tend to be fairly inflexible and are expected to be adhered to.

■ *Can be vague*

Italians tend to be somewhat vague (calculated nonchalance) as a negotiating tactic. To indicate a sense of urgency plays into their hands.

■ *Relationships important*

Italians feel that internal relationships and business contacts are very important. While they are open to outsiders, they don't adapt their customs and outlook for them. To do business with Italians, it is important to get to know them and build their trust. It can be difficult getting tasks completed if no relationship has been built.

Money is seen as the way to pursue art, culture, leisure and a more enjoyable lifestyle, not as an end in itself.

■ *Contracts*

Italians generally don't like detailed agreements and contracts with lots of rules.

United States

■ *Dislike haggling*

Americans tend to be very competitive and want to get the best deal, but they tend to do very little haggling. Negotiating is usually a matter of finalizing the price and settling the details. Americans do not usually anticipate long-term negotiations.

■ *Impatient*

Decisions are often made quickly. Not all decisions need to be made by executives; sometimes lower-level managers can make decisions. Sometimes their impatience to complete negotiations can lead Americans to make unnecessary concessions.

Punctuality is important. Americans will seldom be more than a few minutes late to a meeting or negotiation session. They also expect others to be equally punctual.

■ *Like haggling*

Italians particularly like to haggle about price. They are less concerned about delivery, quality or performance (although their workmanship is generally high).

Italians try to get an agreement to their proposals before the meeting if possible. If new ideas are sprung during a meeting, everyone will generally object automatically. So they try to clear proposals with participants first. Opinions must not be imposed but agreed to. A complete consensus is necessary or those not in agreement may undermine the decision. It is also important to give dissenters time to save face and a way to change their minds, perhaps after a caucus.

■ *More casual about time*

Negotiating with Italians can take a lot of patience and flexibility. Italians are among the least punctual people in Europe — assuming they show up at all. Meetings can be postponed minutes before they are scheduled to begin.

Negotiating

United States

■ *Formal agendas*

Americans like formal agendas for negotiating sessions and expect these agendas to be adhered to. They like fast-paced negotiations. Americans are very devoted to schedules, timelines and deadlines.

They also tend to attack issues sequentially, resolving them one issue at a time.

■ *Negotiators*

The people who are negotiating for their company or business have usually been notified by high-level executives beforehand regarding the expected agreement/outcome of the meeting.

■ *More informal*

Italians tend to take a more informal attitude toward negotiations. Agendas are more loose and informal meetings are as important as formal ones. This reflects their view that establishing a business relationship is important.

■ *Negotiators*

Negotiations should ideally be between executives of equivalent rank — decision makers. Middle-level people are used for preliminary negotiations. Higher-level executives enter the negotiation process at a later date when they wish to stress the importance of the business transaction.

U.S. Business Etiquette

- Be punctual. Americans are very time conscious. They also tend to conduct business at a fairly fast pace.

- A firm handshake and direct eye contact is the standard greeting.

- Direct eye contact is very important in business. Not making eye contact implies boredom or disinterest.

- Gift giving is not common. The United States has bribery laws which restrict the value of gifts which can be given.

- The United States is not particularly rank and status conscious. Titles are not used when addressing executives. Americans usually like to use first names very quickly. Informality tends to be equated with equality.

- Business meetings usually start with a formal agenda and tasks to be accomplished. There is usually very little small talk. Participants are expected to express their ideas openly; disagreements are common.

- Permission should be asked before smoking.

- If there is no one to introduce you in a business meeting, you may introduce yourself and present your card.

Italian Business Etiquette

- Italians shake hands when meeting and departing no matter how brief or often the encounter.

- Italians have an easy formality in manners, but courtesy and good manners are highly prized.

- Italians tend to dress formally.

- Italians preserve a sharp distinction between work and private life. If you are invited out socially, it is important to accept to show respect.

- It is important to show great respect to upper management in Italian companies.

- Italians love to smoke and have expresso coffee throughout the day.

- Use professional titles when addressing Italians. If meeting one who has an aristocratic title, use that title at first. It is best to err on the side of being too formal.

- Business cards are an important part of your identity. Have your card translated into Italian on one side.

- Gift giving among business associates is common.

- Except in Milan, Italians do not do a lot of business entertaining.

U.S. Gestures

- Americans tend to stand an arms length away from each other.

- Americans generally respect queues or lines. To shove or push one's way into a line will often result in anger and verbal complaint.

- Beckoning is done by raising the index finger and curling it in and out, or by raising the hand and curling the fingers back toward the body.

- Using the hand and index finger to point at objects or to point directions is common.

- Whistling is a common way to get the attention of someone at a distance.

- "No" is signalled by waving the forearm and hand (palm out) in front and across the upper body, back and forth.

- Americans use the standard OK sign, the V for victory sign and the thumbs up sign.

- Italians tend to be very demonstrative when talking. They like lots of physical contact.

- Italians tend to use close physical distance, talk loudly and poke the other person on the shoulder when conversing.

- An up-and-down nod of the head with the chin high and the eyes closed means no.

- You should take great care when using gestures in Italy; they can mean something other than what you intend. Nonverbal gestures are a common part of the Italian communication style.

- In Italy it is not considered rude to push or shove slightly in crowded public places.

- Italian male friends often hug as a sign of close friendship.

Communication Interferences

Effective communication, both verbal and nonverbal, means that the sending and processing of information between people, countries and businesses is understood, examined, interpreted, and responded to in some way. Any factor that causes a barrier or eliminates the successful transmission of information is defined as a communication interference.

- **Environmental interference** is an actual physical disturbance in the environment such as a power outage, unregulated temperatures, a person or group talking very loudly, etc.

- **Physiological interference** can be a hearing loss, laryngitis, illness, stuttering, neurological or organic deficit, etc.

- **Semantic interference.** We understand a word to have a certain meaning but the other person has a different meaning. Body language and gestures mean different things to different people. This includes confusion of abbreviated organizational jargon and pronunciation. Universal meanings (semantic understanding) are rare.

- **Syntactic interference.** Words are placed in certain order to give our language meaning. If the words are out of order, the meaning may be changed (this includes grammar).

- **Organizational interference.** Ideas being discussed lack sequence and can't be followed.

- **Psychological interference.** Words that incite emotion are used. In any emotional state (positive or negative) emotions need to be diffused in order to communicate effectively.

- **Social interference.** This includes cultural manners that are inappropriate for the country such as accepted codes for dress, business etiquette, communication rules and social activity.

Always become well informed about the customs and culture and get information before you try and do business in another country. Review this book and decide which areas of communication you and your colleagues will have difficulty with in Italy. Anticipate and plan accordingly.

As the visitor to another country, you need to move out of your "comfort zone." Make the people from that country feel comfortable doing business with you.

No one country has a lock on world markets. Fundamental changes have occurred in the world economy in the last decade. New technologies and low labor costs often give nations that once were not major players an advantage. This results in increased competition. Yet international business is vital to any country's prosperity.

Business is conducted by people and the future of any country in a global economy will lie with people who can effectively think and act across ethnic, cultural and language barriers. We need to understand that the differences between nations and cultures are profound. The European-based culture of the United States has very different values and behaviors than other cultures in the world. If you cannot accept and adapt to these differences, you will not succeed.

Companies striving to market their business overseas can become truly successful only when they recognize that the key is operating with sensitivity toward the culture and communication of the other country. Communication cannot be separated from culture and this is true when doing business in other countries.

No flourishing company would present themselves to another company in their own country without researching that company's business culture and then adapting their image to meet the customer's comfort level. It's the same when doing business in another country. You must adapt your image by using your knowledge of effective cultural communication to present a positive public image to the other country.

The first thing is to identify your target audience: clients, customers, suppliers, financial people, government employees and so on. Then you must learn how to effectively communicate with them, and this means learning the culture.

Business failure internationally rarely results from technical or professional incompetence. It is often due to a lack of understanding of what people from other countries want, how they work and so on. This lack of understanding can put a company at a tremendous disadvantage.

Learning the business protocol and practices of the country where you want to do business can give you great leverage. The more you know about the people you do business with, the more successful you can be. Businesspeople need to make every contact they have with a foreign customer or business partner a positive one. Business leaders and managers must rethink the way they do business in the new global marketplace.

To be successful in the global market, you must:

- **Be flexible.** Cultural adaptations are necessary for both countries to get along and do business. Resisting the local culture will only lead to distrust.

- **Be patient.** Adjust your planning. Initiating business in many countries takes a long-range approach and may require two or three years. Anticipate problems and develop alternative strategies.

- **Prepare thoroughly.** Research the country, the organization, the culture and beliefs of the people you will be dealing with.

- **Know your bottom line.** Know exactly what you want from a deal and at what point an agreement is not in your best interest. Know when to walk away.

- **Form relationships.** Encourage getting involved with the new community if you're going to be in the country for a long period.

- **Keep your cool.** Pay attention to the wide range of national, cultural, religious and social differences you encounter.

- **Show respect.** Search for the other side's needs and interests. Accentuate the positive. Don't preach your own beliefs and respect their beliefs.

When you are using this book, review your own beliefs and values about correct business protocol and ethics. Then match these ideas with the business practices and protocol in Italy.

You can contribute to your own success by recognizing that you will have to move out of your own "comfort zone" of doing business into the cultural business zone of Italy in order to develop the rapport necessary to meet the needs of your client or partner. This does not mean you compromise your company's image or product but that you do business following Italy's protocol while there. It's only for a short time that you may be following their rules, and the payoff can be one in which concepts can be sold while still maintaining a consistent image and approach that is culturally appropriate.

Tips: Doing Business in the U.S.

- The United States is a very ethnically diverse country. To do business, it is important to be open to this diversity and to be flexible.

- Americans tend to be very individually oriented and concerned with their own careers. Their first loyalty is to themselves.

- Americans want to be liked. They prefer people who are good team players and want to cooperate.

- Americans value equality and dislike people who are too status or rank conscious.

- Most Americans are open, friendly, casual and informal in their manners. They like to call people by their first names soon after meeting.

- Americans like to come right to the point and are uncomfortable with people who are indirect and subtle. They like a direct and specific "yes" or "no."

- Americans expect people to speak up and give their opinions freely and to be honest in the information they give.

- Americans can be very persistent. When they conclude a business transaction and sign a contract, they expect it to be honored. They do not like people who change their minds later.

Tips: Doing Business in Italy

- Don't jump to conclusions. If you feel offended, frustrated or angry at something said or done, you may have just misunderstood.

- Be patient. Spend some time developing relationships. It takes time to find decision makers. Try to find and approach the decision maker as quickly as possible.

- Take your attorney along when negotiating. Written contracts are considered sacred. Lawyers can assist in defining and understanding details as Italians can often be somewhat vague.

- Preserve a certain formality in all your business dealings; formality as well in dress and in manners. Italians tend to be more conservative than Americans in this respect.

- Do not assume all Italians are alike. Italy is an extremely varied country.

- Being cultivated is very important. Italians respect people who are well read and know something about their history. Education is very important in determining class distinctions. They are especially impressed with degrees in the sciences.

Quick Tips: Doing Business in Italy

- Italians can seem frantic, slightly inefficient, a trifle disorganized and in a hurry to be late. Because of this, it can sometimes take longer to get things done.

- Italy is an inward-looking country; Italians do not readily adapt to others' ways of doing things. You must adjust to their culture and slow down to their tempo to do business with them.

- Italian business meetings may be very casual. They like to spend time getting acquainted and don't always get down to business right away. They enjoy small talk and especially like to talk about their families. They also like it if you bring pictures of your family and talk about them. Small gifts for children are always acceptable.

- American men meeting Italian women, either socially or professionally, will be expected to either shake her hand, kiss it or receive a kiss on the cheek. Let the woman determine what she wants and respond accordingly.

- Although Italians will socialize in business by going to dinner, they don't really talk business. Eating is for enjoyment. Keep your drinking in moderation.

- Italians have a very laid-back lifestyle. Career achievement is highly valued but not as important as their relationship with their family. They believe that long hours and business trips interfere with enjoyment. They may be inclined to work less hard in order to devote themselves to their families.

- Fluent English speakers are not prevalent in Italy. Italians do a lot of smiling and waving of their arms. They put a lot of emphasis on non-verbal communication. And although they can appear to be very nonchalant, it is very important to really listen, watch the nonverbal communication and try to figure out what they really want.

Common Phrases

Good morning	Buon giorno
Good afternoon	Buon giorno/Buona sera
Good evening	Buona sera
My name is	Mi chiamo
What's your name	Come se chiama?
Pleased to meet you	Placere di conoscerla
How are you	Come sta
Fine, thank you	Bene, grazie
You are welcome	Prego
Please	Per favore/Per placere
Thank you	Grazie
Yes/No	Si/No
Goodbye	Arrivederci
Mr./Mrs./Miss	Signor/Signora/Signorina

Available in this series:

Business China

Business France

Business Germany

Business Japan

Business Mexico

Business Taiwan

Business Korea

Business Italy

For more information, please contact:

Sales and Marketing Department
NTC Publishing Group
4255 West Touhy Avenue
Lincolnwood, IL 60646
798-679-5500